Naked

TO THE

Wind

ALLYENE PALMER

Order this book online at www.trafford.com
or email orders@trafford.com

Most Trafford titles are also available at major online book retailers.

Cover Design by:
Sue Nowlin
The Master's Studio
Jackson, Wyoming

Print information available on the last page.

ISBN: 978-1-4907-5220-4 (sc)
ISBN: 978-1-4907-5219-8 (e)

Trafford rev. 05/19/2015

 www.trafford.com

North America & international
toll-free: 1 888 232 4444 (USA & Canada)
fax: 812 355 4082

Contents

Dedication

To my husband Richard,
who has always been dedicated to the
proposition that this book is worth
doing; and to the memory of
artist and author Mary Back, who
was my dear friend and encourager
through tough times.

Acknowledgments

Some of these poems have been published in *Living Water, Writing at Wyoming, Wyoming Writers, The Anglican Digest, The Wyoming Churchman* and *The American Poetry Anthology 1986*.

The poem *"Jonah and Me"* won first prize in the religious division of the 1986 American Poetry Society competition. *"Wyoming"* placed third in the Wyoming Writers annual poetry competition in 1987.

Places

Somehow the heart picks
A particular place to love
Above all others; and yet
A distant country
Calls. Sometimes
A little town passed through
Creates an ache,
A yearning - it is sad
To give up all the places
Never known.

Wyoming Lovesong

I've seen high mountain meadows lying golden in the sun. I've seen deep shadowed valleys where crystal waters run. I've seen the glory of the sunset painted on the western sky, and the yawning purple canyons where the swooping nighthawks fly. I've sat upon a sun-warmed rock to watch the squirrels play, heard the bugle of the regal elk on a crisp October day. On the sunny side of a haystack I've sat and read a book in February warmth brought in by the welcome, good Chinook. I've smelled rain out on the prairie, heard the Hahn's Peak's lonesome wail; seen dappled shadows moving on a pine-needle-cushioned trail. I've heard the rain-drops' rhythm on a tent in high cow-camp, played "solo" in the evening by the light of a coal-oil lamp. I've heard some tough old cowhands tell their tales of times long gone. I've washed my face in an ice-cold creek in the rosy mountain dawn.

I wish that some way I could tell you about this land I've loved so long. I love this old Wyoming where the wind blows free and strong; where nothing is built so high as to block the sky that I can see, and the moving, shifting, changing clouds are part of the scenery.

Not Even Grief

A vacant house sits high on a barren hill
Where no grass grows; rocks surround, sparce straggles of sagebrush
Clutch tenaciously at sterile ground.
Two gnarled cottonwoods
Stand, gaunt guardians,
More branches bare than leafing,
Only a token acknowledgment give
To season's change.
The old house sits with sagging porches,
Windows staring lifelessly
And sightlessly, while aimless idle winds
Pluck ceaselessly and make no difference
To this old house which just is there, and is.

Too many years of drouth, a cloudburst flood,
Too many buffetings by tearing blasts
Have drained this house of heart and love, have emptied it.
Not even grief remains, to give it life.

Seasons

Springtime valleys, sunlit green with forget-me-not coverlets of astonishing blue; daisies of lavender, yellow, white, Indian paintbrush of scarlet hue.

Summertime valleys, emerald velvet with blossoming cloverfields silverbright; orange tiger lily, purple phlox, Queen Anne's lace in pristine white.

Autumntime valleys, soft green-gray bounded with goldenrod catching light; silverdollar seedpods, milkweed, too, bronze at evening and ghostly at night.

Wintertime valleys, dappled in blue, carpeted with snowdrifts stitched with pine; pink glow in the sunrise, and deep in the sunset, burgundy wine.

Mountain Storm

Deep down canyon walls the thunder booms. Lightning plays a light-show; shadows leap. It is a time for wonder, not for sleep.

We lie in awe within our sheltered rooms. I think about the rabbits in the grass, the field mice cuddled softly in the nest; I wonder, will the storm disturb their rest, and do they tremble, too, until it pass? And deer down in the meadow, do they shrink, startle with each sharp and brilliant flash, and cower at the thunder's roll and crash?

Their timid hearts may pound as mine, I think. I snuggle close to you, and gladly cling for comfort to your flesh; it makes me warm and lulls the fears engendered by the storm. I wish such warmth for every living thing.

Upper Country

There is a time in the upper country where the little streams have their headings when the winter snows begin to melt and leave their icy beddings of banked-high fleece beneath the pines, to start their springtime wending down the rocky mountainsides, and come together, blending; make themselves a larger stream, flowing still, and with more rigor until another with them join and make them fuller, bigger.

Now on the lower, calmer banks of the wooded, full Wind River, I feel my heart overflow with thanks to those streams, who strength do give her. My heart is full, up to the banks, like the strongly flowing, seaward going, life-bestowing, wooded, full Wind River.

Wyoming

Wyoming; your very name tells the story
Of restless, haunting winds, and skies that reach
From one far bright horizon to the other.
Of the pungent, permeating scent of sagebrush; each
Syllable of your singing name, Wyoming,
Evokes a vision of reaching, stretching plain,
And I can hear in it the creaking, creaking
Wheels of a long-forgotten wagon train.
Magic name, magic names within a name, Wyoming;
Sweetwater, bright sparkling crystal liquid to slake
A burning thirst that grew across the endless miles
Of a rise beyond a rise beyond a rise, and make
A dream-driven man take heart once more, Wyoming;
Your waters were hidden and often hard to find
And mirages came from the burning, glassy sky
To taunt a tortured, thirst-tormented mind.
Fort Washakie; a name that holds a tribute, Wyoming,
Monument to a man with a greater, stronger soul,
Than was ever thought to live in untamed country
Among a nomadic, unlearned, simple people whose whole
Existence depended, when life was centered, Wyoming,
Round the rusty, shaggy, plodding buffalo. Buffalo fed the peaceful
people of Washakie, the Shoshone;
Quiet people who live where the Big and Little Wind flow.
Oh, the names that sing within your boundaries, Wyoming;
Meeteetse and Sundance and Crazy Woman Creek.

They tell of the dreams and the death of dreams, Wyoming,
Of the men and women who crossed the plains to seek
A better land, a better life, Wyoming.
And for some, the prairie skies were what they sought.
Brave souls have crossed this boundless reach, Wyoming,
And fears have been overcome, and battles fought,
And some have stayed and loved you long, Wyoming,
Your purple mountain peaks and shadowed valleys deep;
And some went on to find a new horizon
But left a loved one in your sod to sleep.
The sound of your name still sings to me, Wyoming,
It calls to me and I hear it wherever I go,
And I know it will ever draw me back, Wyoming,
To the blue-skied land where the clear, clean waters flow.

Rainy Daybreak

Today the earth is new. It rained last night. Frayed-edged, ragged clouds are drifting by, subtle as a whisper, soft as a sigh. A sweeter freshness glows in day's gray light. Bird-sounds are subdued.

Though yesterday they rose at dawn to fill the early air with loud and joyous twitterings, to share sun's rising, celebrate each golden ray, today birds sing a different song of praise, a quiet hymn to greet the paler morn. Flowers, like old clothes much washed and often worn, adorn a vista softened down with grays. And I, an early riser, inclined to greet each newborn day with plans and great delight, in rainy times relax and think I might at slower pace, with love, some lesser task complete.

Mountains

Mountains move with seasons. I have seen them move, have marked how every year, near and softly-contoured they appear in summer, wearing warm and golden green; but when winter snows begin to pile in drifts, all sharply blue and deeply cold, when frost and ice their rocky peaks enfold, define the pines' and aspens' rank and file, then from my window I again perceive them distant and unfriendly. Until spring I grieve.

Country Prayer

Father, thank you for sounds of life-beholding springtime in the country; immobile cattle intercept the strengthened sun, winter-hidden fowl come forth and blink, stretched out red legs, spread their wings and sing out their joy. It is the glory of new life, to hear your gift of barnsong rising to the spring.

Father, thank you for the scents of life-exuding springtime in the country; tender shoots emerge to taste the rain. Winter-forbidden trees assume a shy green blush, loose tight-curled buds, flex cramped roots and exhale sweetness. It is the glory of new life, to sniff your gift of leafscent rising to the spring.

Father, thank you for the sights of life-affirming springtime in the country; night-foaled colts flip corrugated tails; new-dropped calves in fields aspraddle stand, test clovering air, unlock knee joints and leap and run. It is the glory of new life, to see your gift of beastbirth rising to the spring.

Father, thank you for the touch of life-releasing springtime in the country; cold-prisons unbarred in first-felt tremor loose winter-stiffened spirits, sun-elate unfolding, tremulous petals to warmth and urge to grow. It is the glory of new life, to feel your gift of soulstretch rising to the spring.

O Hear The Call To Summer

O hear the call to summer, hear larks down in the meadow; tree-frogs singing in the swamp; far-off cattle lowing, horse-bells, echoed faintly from the pasture's lower end.

Hear the trilling chorus of blackbirds, bees humming in unison, gathering while the earth is full and comfort overflows. O hear the call to summer, hear and heed the call intently; too soon it is too late to hear the urgent call to summer.

Winter Day
in Laramie

Snow piles high in drifts to the windowsill, frozen to crisp escarpment; frost crystals glister in the air. With breath of life visible, the town is imprisoned, caught, stands surrounded by cold that assumes proportions and becomes a tangible.

Functions slow. As paces ease, people relax into a fellowship of extremity.

Early Fall

Who lives at the foot of the mountain knows summer's time is fleeting, knows in the midst of August heat a rainy day can bring a nipping breath of autumn and a fretting whining wind to nag until summer is on her way out and winter can come in.

Summer

These are the moments for expectant listening in quiet contemplation; these are the days for looking in stillness. There is a glistening of darting ripples surfacing a shadowed stream to see, and a vast cathedral hush to hear; christening of a newborn summer.

These are not the times for rush and hurrying; even forest shadows quietly lie, and stilled, forgetful of the springtime flutter-flurrying; the leafy minuet no longer calls to dance. Come, rest a while; too soon will come the scurrying restless winds of autumn.

Cow Camp

Have you ever been in a cow camp at the breaking of the dawn in the frosty nip of mountain air, a pot of coffee on and the smell of bacon frying, driving thoughts of sleep away; splashed your face with icy water and turned to greet the day?

Have you seen the thrusting mountains in the pink of early morn, with your eyes full of joy and wonder at the sight of a new day born?

Did you ever walk a woodland trail with sunlight shining through and dappled shadows moving in a pattern ever new? And the sun-distilled pine scent, and the hushing of the breeze and the everlasting whisper of the rustling aspen trees?

Did you ever watch the thunderheads begin to boil and churn along the far horizon; feel the sun beat down and burn, and hear the distant rumble as the thunder starts to speak and to echo and reecho from peak to rocky peak?

Have you ever stopped to listen and to feel the quickened breeze and to hear the rain's glad patter as it greets the waiting trees?

Have you watched it swiftly darken as the clouds blot out the sun and see tall trees their branches toss ere yet the storm's begun?

Did you ever lie in a tent and drowse as the rain came pattering down and the thunder crashed and the lightning sparked on a nearby ridge's crown?

Did you ever stand when the storm had passed and smell the freshened air and take a deep breath, and feel that the rain had washed away every care?

Have you watched the shadows lengthen and the twilight settle in, heard the hush that falls over the forest ere the soft night sounds begin?

Or sat beside a campfire and watched a log burn bright as leaping shadows played hide and seek with the dancing, golden light? And after the fire burned down to ash did you ever watch the sky and see a bright star impaled upon a pine tree standing high?

Have you watched as its companions came forth in the velvet night to trace their mysterious patterns in myriads dots of light? And did you feel, as you watched them move how sometime you'd like to try to decipher the great eternal Truth emblazoned in the sky, but found somehow, before you knew, your eyelids closed in sleep to wake at the dawn with your soul refreshed from a slumber profound and deep?

A day and night in a cow camp is enough to make you whole, to bring you peace, and cleanse your heart, and rest your weary soul.

People

Where else can we find ourselves
except in the persons around us?
God made us to be
In His company
And blessed with all those who
Surround us.

Friends

(For Darolyn and Viola)

Not alike except in this: they love me.
No matter what, they're for me; why they do and are
I will never know -- it goes so far
Back in time through things we shared when we
Were younger much and had our dreams and plans,
And years and wars and men and babies came and went
And times were hard or easy. Pots and pans
And diapers, and floors to scrub -- it was the same
For all of us; not in detail, but in the main.
Each of us loved, and gave, and suffered pain,
And somehow found a way to love again.

What I know is this: I made it through
The joys and pains of life because I knew
I had the trust and love and friendship of these two.

Bag Lady

Rehearsing, mutters
Plots against her, how they
Did what they did.

Tears in channels,
Courses of grey-brown
Wrinkles run.

This is hers,
Treasures scrabbled for,
Scavenged things.

Plastic-bagged
Intrepid angry journey,
Holding on.

Jonah And Me

Now and again I spend a few days
Sitting in the belly of a whale
Yelling, "I won't!"
Or a-sulk in the shade
Of a temporary vine. In my time
I have begrudged my share of Ninevehs
Their second chance. Hell's elevators would scarcely hold
Consignments I'd have sent
Had I been God. Thank God:
He's slow to move, quick to forgive,
And has more care for sinning souls than I;
More compassion for several thousand silly souls
Who don't know their right hand from their left,
And many cattle to boot! O, God,
Be a little hard of hearing, I pray,
When I sit under a wilted vine
And complain about your mercy. Amen.

Heartbeat

"I took a deep breath and listened to the old brag of my heart. I am, I am, I am." Sylvia Plath (1932-1963). American poet who died a suicide at the age of 31.

Ah, but "I am" has no meaning to me;
I cannot claim
For myself an existence apart from Him
Who created me.
I AM is He, not me, and even the beat of
my heart.
Depends on Him.
O heart, do not brag "I am,"
Boasting will not keep your beat alive
Nor set the pace of your beating.
Say rather of the God who made you,
"HE IS. Say,
"Because of Him I sojourn here
And, if He wills, I may for a little
while, and then
Be with Him forever because HE IS
And my being is in Him."
O my heart, say only that.

Pan's Advice

Son, life is worth living, and love is worth giving, though you may think life stinks and love has expired. Most times I'm your father and sometimes your mother but in bad times between us, I'm God's wrath on your head. Son, throw back your shoulders and tighten your belly; keep your mind open, your heart open, too; keep your eyes looking, your ears always hearing; look out for the women and poor orphan children, and remember to tuck in your gut and your chin.

Old Indians

Row of Indians sit on curb;
Eyes opaque, unreadable,
Look out across smelly asphalt
At red brick walls and neon.
Row of Indians sit on curb;
Faces expressionless,
Windows with shades drawn
Concealing sorrow inside
(As house where death has come.) Row of Indians sit on curb;
Bear the sorrow of seeing noisy cars
Where once the buffalo grazed,
Asphalt in place of grass. Old Indians soon will go the way
Of graygreen grass and vanished buffalo.

Garbo

"What I said was, I just want to be left alone." Greta Garbo.

She did not really want to be alone;
the words she spoke had more to them than that.
She knew the perils of a public life,
she feared the power of the written word. Let me alone -- I think it
meant just this:
Don't analyze my life. And she was right.
To scrutinize her years by day and week, to miniaturize or magnify
at will,
to probe and pry and paw through private things,
customs and thoughts and habits that were hers,
idiosyncracies they would reveal,
explain her in a way to satisfy
themselves, and titillate the world; to
construct of her an image, and to claim
for it what should be hers alone.
Then what could she believe? Somehow I know
that she was right. "Let me alone," she said,
and meant, perhaps, "Let God say who I am."

Denver Lovesong

Annie-Fannie, how I love
the way you rule your street;

Your loose and too-big men's black shoes
on rough-heeled sockless feet.

I love the way your coat is long
in front, and short in back.
And colored brown, or is it green? (or maybe rusty black.)

I love the way your shapeless hat
sits your gray-black-yellow hair;
How contumelious the way
you mash it down to keep it there!

Annie-Fannie, I believe,
two wrinkles more that hat could be
Screwed-down upon your dear old head
in perpetuity.

She knelt with the other women, praying, blue cotton kerchief on her head. In the east, the morning sky was graying. Her lips were pale and her eyes were red: her heartbeat shook her in her dread. Will they be found alive or dead? "Oh, God, not dead with those last screaming words I said."

The mine, the mine is dark and deep and women lonely vigil keep; for sons and husbands and brothers weep. "Killer mine, give up your prey. Send back our men. Don't let this Easter be the day we weep again."

"Hey Rosa! Get the lazy ass outa bed! It's a workin' day, come on!" Was it only yesterday, one dawn -- last dawn? "Damn!" she spat, hissed at him like an angry cat. "You think I don't know what you're at? You, with your smart alec Irish friend, makin' eyes at that skinny Irene; makin' her think she's some kinda queen, makin' her think you got money to spend! Come stompin' home late, make noise at the gate, and old lady Gorski knows I gotta wait and keep your supper for you on a plate, so now it's Rosa, get your lazy ass outa bed? Tony, I hate you! I wish you dead!"
A shrilling, angry Sicilian wife has a tongue like a whip or a well-honed knife.

The word went out at a little past five; a cave-in at the mine. "They don't know if they're alive."

All night long, the women stayed, stood and waited -- knelt and prayed; of them all, Rosa most afraid.

Rosa raised her head and looked about with unseeing eyes at the deserted town. A ray of rising sun reached out and gilded windows with yellow light, edged scarred hills with a halo bright; banished the last of the long, long night. A morning breeze fluttered the women's dresses and playfully lifted a lock of hair on Rosa's forehead. She did not feel its caresses nor the touch of the moving, morning air.

"They're coming up!" Is it life -- or death? Dread preceded the lift like an icy breath. "They live! We found them!" A joyous shout from those who waited, and the men coming out.
"Tony, Tonio, you all right?"
"Well, I'm hungry as hell, in the mine all night! What the hell you doin', down here lookin'? Get your ass on home and get to cookin'!"

"Damn you, Tony! I wish --," Rosa bowed her head then raised it. "-- you'd say 'I love you' instead."

The miners, the miners are wild and rough; to work in the mines they have to be tough. Rosa will weep again, Rosa will hiss, she'll snarl and she'll swear again at Tony, no doubt; if he comes home late and staggers at the gate she'll glare again at him with her eyes full of hate.

On that Easter she was silent for a husband's kiss, knew the joy of Resurrection. One day achieved perfection. The men in the mine were out!

Washakie And Roberts

As one good man knows the heart of another, a loving priest could wish to be brother to an Indian chief whose heart was wild with pain; Washakie, man of wisdom, was so loved by John Roberts, man of God.

Washakie's son had been gunned down in a wild saloon in the white man's town, killed in a drunken brawl. Great compassion for Washakie, man of wisdom, filled John Roberts, man of God.

He would kill each man he met until brought down as he walked the trail from his camp into town. To avenge his beloved son Washakie vowed in passion; word was sent from Washakie, man of wisdom, to John Roberts, man of God.

The chief was filled with sorrow and anger, but the priest, most fully aware of the danger, somehow was able to start. To meet and speak once again with Washakie, man of wisdom, went John Roberts, man of God.

In his mountain lodge the great chief prayed to his gods to help him keep the vow he had made, as in the valley below, so the other humbly prayed, and then toward Washakie, man of wisdom, climbed John Roberts, man of God.

Into Washakie's lodge at midnight John Roberts came; in love he simply spoke the great chief's name. "This thing that you have said, you know it is not good to do." To Washakie, man of wisdom, spoke John Roberts, man of God.

"Your people and mine need the counsel that you give. You are a great wise chief, and you must live. Is blood all that your grief requires? Then let me give my own." Then Washakie, man of wisdom, looked long at John Roberts, man of God.

Eyes still aflame with rage, the chief pondered, as in the depths of his proud heart he wondered; what moves this white man's heart to wish to give his life? Sighing, Chief Washakie, man of wisdom, asked John Roberts, man of God.

All night John Roberts spoke of the great God above who sent his Son to die because of his great love for white man and Indian alike; and as morning dawned in the eastern sky, great Washakie, man of wisdom, was baptized by John Roberts, man of God.

And so it came about that these two great men brought together in peace were friends again: more than friends, indeed, true brothers. Love flowed instead of blood, between Washakie, man of wisdom, and John Roberts, man of God.

Jimmy Hill

"Too many lines cross in this house,"
said Jimmy Hill,
sitting at my cluttered kitchen table
drinking coffee,
cowboy hat pushed back
on his head,
booted, spurred, and ready
to ride on.
Shoshone cowboy friend -- Jimmy Hill
saw his brother die of pneumonia
after an all night peyote meeting
in a wickiup back of Crowheart.

Where Esther was was always a place
Where you could go and be warmed,
Be comforted, be fed. Esther was
A keeper of the fire, a baker of bread,
A loving arm, a straight-on look.
When Esther took a crying infant
On her ample lap, warmed its blanket
In the wood-stove's oven and
Wrapped it tight about the squirming babe,
Captured the agitated arms and blue-cold hands,
Its squalling ceased and the screamer slept
Content. (Babies tend to fright when their flailing arms escape and
beat the air
As if in flight.) It always was
To the place where Esther was we mothers took
Our newborns to be seen, approved
And paid attention to. Where Esther was
Was always a place where when we came
The coffeepot gurgled and perked,
A teakettle sang and something smelled good
In the oven roasting and baking,
Where quiet reigned, and steadiness,
Where girl-children were called "Sister"
And took it as something special, and boys
Were mostly always "Brother" and felt like men.

Esther could carry a toddler
On a pillow on the saddle before her
Horseback on a mountain trail;
Could manage its care in cow-camp, fish for trout
And help with the branding, too.
Esther could stir up a bowl of batter,
Cook it up into hotcakes or waffles with
One baby on her hip and another on her apron strings;
Could cope with a pet piglet asleep
In her basket of ironing, could dispose
Of a dead mouse deposited at her feet
By Toby the family cat as proof that he
Was continuing to earn his keep, and assure him
That he was indeed a magnificent, heroic beast.
When Esther died, it seemed we all stood
Naked to the wind, our shelter blown away,
And yearned for walls and fire and solid ground,
For something to hold us together, to wrap us,
To contain us, like babies who beat the air
With frantic, flailing arms.

Indian Hospital 1941

Tomorrow, perhaps, my baby will be born; tomorrow or another day soon. Very soon. Tonight I lie immobilized 'neath sterile sheets of white under the orders of the government-provided doctor to the Shoshone people, in the government hospital; quiet rigidly-regulated institution where an Indian might go to die; where an Indian girl gives birth to a baby, and stares unblinkingly at a starched nurse who disapproves with cold eyes, of Indian girls who, though unmarried, do not cry out in childbed pain; who are more embarrassed at being in white hands in a scrubbed-out Indian hospital than at giving birth to fatherless babies. What baby was ever fatherless among the Shosone? (Indian women smile behind their hands; Lucy-Dora Shinjoe got herself a baby down in the brush with Robert Lame Bull.) Tomorrow, or perhaps in the day following, my baby will be born. He will have a father who will escort me in state throught the doors of this kindly-intentioned and benevolent institution and take me home. Tonight, gown-swathed and bored I lie, nervous, a little, perhaps. Eyes look in at me from the door; eyes of an inquisitive deer set in the round, brown face of a child, outlined with a straight-cut, smooth-combed fall of hair, reflecting purple and blue, like a crow's feather on a fence at noon. What is your name, little sister? Don't run away. (Will you run? Will you run? Oh, stay.) I'm named Olive. (What unreflecting eyes you have, little Olive; the better to hide your judgment, I suppose.) What is wrong with your legs, little sister? (Poor twice-hurt legs; ricket-bowed and now bound round with white, encasing lengths of cotton gauze, and tightly taped.)

Deer eyes move cautiously closer: I fell in the fire and burned. (Don't let the lurch of your heart frighten the child away.) The doctor will be back tomorrow. See, I only can slide my feet.

(Oh, lame Shoshone baby, if I held my arms out how quickly those feet would glide down the painful corridor, and away.) And what is the name of your friend, Olive? Now, four bright forest eyes instead of two; this head wearing an oh, so clean white turban wrapped around. She, she not my friend; she Arapahoe. Her name Mary Deer Fly. She has other bed in my room. Poor Mary Deer Fly; how has she hurt her head? Four round eyes are kind and amused. They look long at me, and Olive will be spokesman. Oh, she not hurt her head, white lady. Mary Deer fly, she got bugs. Suddenly I am tired. Suddenly I am so very, very tired. Good night, Olive. Slide your burned-up, ricket-twisted legs back down the hall to your room. Good night, Mary Deer Fly. Bring your bug-infested head back in the morning. Good night, little daughters of enemy peoples; God give you each a peaceful night, and grant the same to me.

Starched skirt rustles at midnight; I startle. My heart-pound is a drum in the quiet room. Soft, sibilant noises in the next room; it is a sun porch, and the window opens to my bed. Agnes Running Water, wake up, your baby has died. Poor baby has been rattling and rattling with pneumonia. The rattle has stopped and now a rustling of skirts, muffled voices, footsteps hurrying, hurrying up the hall. Quiet settles around again. If I could, I would cry for Agnes Running Water and the poor baby, dead in the night.

Afterthought 1962

I stand in the icy wind for these few moments, and watch as a giant machine with massive jaws snatches great bites of earth from the ground in the town where I grew up. Laramie, Wyoming; it is a small town and has changed much in twenty years. This is the spot where the old post office stood: and standing here, I remember another day. We had walked along together and this is the place where we stopped to talk a moment, before you went your way and I went mine, Andre. I had not lived enough to love you, then; my world was small and bounded by myself. I liked you and thought you were funny with your mobile monkey face, clever mouth cornered with eagerness to laugh; merry, triangular eyes. Your antic tricks were fun; I could not care. It was the year of our Lord One thousand, nine hundred and thirty-eight. You were a Polish Jew, born in China. Only you could know what that meant, to be a Polish Jew, born in China; young, and a man, in that Damocletian year. You knew. You were here to grow your wings; you had to fly. You were an avenging hawk, and the watchful hunter stood waiting in China, and I was very young. We stood on this corner, that crystal-shard day, talking. You were a clown with a red nose and we were happy, careless. Only for an instant you grew serious; told me what you knew. Your words, sliding down the bright, impenetrable mirror of incomprehension, slipped to the sidewalk and lay between us for these more than twenty years. Forgive, Andre. You lie dead in your grave in China and it is another day; I met you too soon and know you too late. At last, Andre . . . . hello.

Mother

We float across the valleys of her mind
like cloud-shadows, mist-memories
of a past long left behind:
she knew us once (she thinks) and tries
to bring us into focus in the now,
this ever-present now, this
undecipherable time or space or place
where half-thoughts come and go
and anger flares and bursts
like fireworks; a meteor-shower
of ugly words and railing against
(what was it? She forgets.)
We grieve. She has not died, and yet
she has to us -- and we, to her.

Bubba's Song

Heartaches and rain go together, gray is the color of pain. My heart hurts as much as a heart can, feels as cold as the falling rain.

Heartaches and rain go together, and they both feel weary and sad. This is the lonesomest day of my life, the worst heartache that I've ever had.

Heartaches and rain go together, and they both go with thinking of you. You left me and heartaches came running; I'm hurting, it's raining, I'm blue.

Heartaches and rain go together, gray is the color of pain. I never thought that you'd leave me, and now it's raining again.

Kaleidoscope

A baby cries in his mother's arms, grey-pink blanket rumpled. She (the mother) looks around with weary, sleep-blurred eyes. Her skirt and blouse are crumpled. Soiled. Her hands tremble in an agony of tiredness as she balances her baby on her arm, fumbles in her purse for some coins to pay for her coffee. An old man in baggy trousers, rheumy-eyed, with knotted hands, sits beside her at the counter clicking his false teeth. Thirty-five other sleepy souls occupy the other thirty-five counter stools, and the utilitarian booths of the bus-stop-coffee-shop are filled while other milling people wait. Fluorescent lights overhead cast a too-bright unshadowed brilliance over this pot-pourri of human imperfection; bad complexions, unpressed clothing, disarray of hair. Two young black soldiers laugh and banter, toss a coin to see who will pay to play the gaudy, blaring juke-box.

Snapping, pettish waitresses scurry, under the lights that etch lines of strain and impatience into their night-time faces.
2 a.m. at the bus-station. Half a hundred weary people moving their troubles -- San Francisco to Chicago; half hundred more to L.A. from Detroit.

Uncle Willie's Lament

Any fool knows a good woman will love you as long as she's got any hope; any fool knows a good woman won't hang you unless you furnish the rope!

And any fool ought to know about the other kind, the kind who'll take a man and rob him blind; who'll bring her own rope and hang him high 'cause she don't care.

Any fool knows a good woman has mercy; she don't want to cause you pain. She'll believe your word when you tell her you're sorry, and take you back again.

And any fool ought to know about the other kind, who'll tell you she loves you and then change her mind; who'll never give an inch, but always takes; who'll squeeze a fool's heart until it breaks, 'cause she don't care.

I'm some kind of fool and I want to tell you that I'm feeling mighty sad 'cause I once had a woman who really loved me and I treated her mighty bad.

I gave up that good woman for one who just used me; left a sweet little woman for one who abused me; who hurt me and cursed me and left me blue, and believe me, fool, she'll do the same to you 'cause she don't care.

Meditation On A War Crimes File

Rachel's daughter, you were no cold-proud Vashti at Shushan. Your gentle eyes were, like the pools at the edges of a river, reed-shadowed; yet, your inheritance, star-christened loveliness of a queen, could not defer destiny for a father who must have seen in deathly dread that in you which so would kindle lust of death, not life, in glittering eyes of men who stood in arrogance of power, occupiers of prominence. An ancient edict restated flared: you, shy and lovely daughter of this patient, star-doomed Mordecai, no sovereign intervention claimed; a thousand desert wanderings were not rehearsal enough for this long trip to Buchenwald, no hate-erected scaffold yet awaited this later Haman.

Random Meanderings

Sometimes you have to stop and think;
then life gets so beautiful
you can barely hold the wonder
of being.

Discovery

Wrinkles, O my God!
and the thickening
of waist, the slowed-up steps
of elderly women -- I
would not have lived so long;
to tell tiresome tales to bored children
and forget
how many times I'd lived them over
in their ears.
"Spare me, life;
I do not want your ravelled-out
end-fringes."

I said that -- but
made that journey quicker than
I meant:
now my mother's face
inhabits my mirror,
surprising me.
Ah, well -- the wind still blows,
beloved mountains stand,
and scent of sage and pine
still fill the air.

Our Motto

"In God We Trust," so our coins say,
And yet we do not live that way:
We trust in luck, and what is funny,
More than anything else, we trust in money!

Cricket

Come, make your home with me.
My hearth is yours, your little song
Will comfort me, and melancholy hours
Will pass; my ticking clock will chime
And you in rhythmic time will chirp
Your cheery little ditty just for me.
Together we will while away
Winter's dark and cold, and in the spring
My heart will sing again. But you
Will be gone. I'll miss you then.

Potential

Mock-fierce, spitting kitten,
Your wrath is absurdity:
I laugh at
Your claim to fierceness, I tease you.
It would be strange to fear
Your playful rage.
You could not possibly become a tiger;
And yet
It is too late to run.

Encounter

Once
When I was a child,
I felt God looking at me,
Delighting in me,
LOVE!
And in the dusk of a summer
Evening
I saw the beauty of
a star
in the translucent sky;
the delicate black
tracery
of trees, a lacy
pattern
and a thin crescent moon;
my soul rejoiced in it
and God
SPOKE TO ME.
HE SAID: I like it, too,
AND I LIKE YOU!

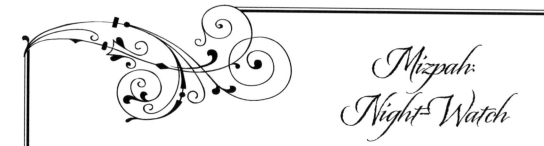

Mizpah: Night Watch

But of course you watch between us all with eyes that see our inmost selves, our minds, our hearts, and all that shows and doesn't show . . . and in the end there will be justice, there will be equity. Examine me, O God, and open me. Make me desire your compassion for every man more passionately than I care for justice.

Help me ever deeply comprehend the knowledge that YOU ARE, and set my soul to that understanding -- that I cease to resent injustice, even for those whom I love. "Unjust, unfair!" is the cry of my soul but still I want to know, I need to know, I KNOW how insignificant unfair is, or fair -- a child's cry, because of course you watch between us all and it all finally comes to rest in you. Peace, then, to my soul.

Upon Being Rejected By a Squirrel

What fraction of totality of human form or feature is impressed upon the vision of this scolding woodland creature who chatters his defiance of my friendship-meant approach as though his own prerogatives I might be here to poach? I see him in entirety; his bright-black, busy eyes are rounded and distended in his fear and his surprise; his whiskers are aquiver and his frantic tail is jerking with the intermittent force behind his fussy "cherk-cherk-cherking." I see all of the squirrel that there is for me to see, but the squirrel, I am thinking, sees but a part of me and understands still less.

I loom on his horizon, not so much figure as event; to him I seem vast shadow cast across the firmament. I threaten his existence in some fearful, unknown way, I am a pall of darkness on the sunshine of his day, and still his minute courage serves to keep and hold him fast; he twitches and he trembles, but does not allow me past this line he has, in reasoning that only he can know, decided is the line past which I shall not dare to go. I wonder if we sometimes seem as dear and as absurd to him who tries to reassure and reach us with His word in our own wilderness.

The Word

Love: What a nice round sound it has,
this word -- easy to mouth. Love: Lips speak it tremblingly,
or forcefully or prayerfully or even
in contempt, harshly -- grating
over old wounds. Love: the Word which once
Spoke Itself, and all Creation
leaped forth to hear.

That's All

Love and fresh air
and empty spaces
in dresser drawers and calendars;
an occasional full moon,
especially in October;
a song I've loved
whistled in the distance,
an old plaid scarf,
beautiful shoes,
tea and buttered toast,
raggedy home-canned peaches,
Willa Cather and rain
and open fires
are what I need.

What I want is just
sometime to spend a month
exploring Prince Edward Island.

The Shop

Come in and look around; who knows what treasures you may find; stashed in boxes, slung on shelves, hung on hooks or spread on dusty tables. Come in and be enchanted; here are relics of other eras, other lives; moldy lampshades, cracked leather boxes--an ivory fan with ribbons frayed. See the woolen skirt, buttons (velvet) all the way down the front.

Gift of Life

What grace, what overwhelming grace this is,
that I should be;
that from those out of whose flesh
I was conceived,
amid all the whirl and touch
and dance away
of human encounter,
by some specificity should be ordained
this one, this very one
particular melding of ovum and sperm,
this me.
O giver of life who brought me out
from not-being
into being,
you by whose ordinance my soul
became enfleshed,
out of all random possibilities
uniquely one,
engrace me, Lord,
that I might love deeply and forever
the gift, the Giver of Gifts,
and in grateful awe and wonder,
be me.

Ennui

Monstrous legacy of boredom
crowding
through the beating of the day
what brings forth intrusion
mocking monotony
when does it end by night
what right of way
will halt
the willful up and down procession.

(Stop,
full stop and silence
and amen.)

Country Blues

Watery blue skim milk aslosh in old gray-blue tin lard pail. Mountain lake blue mirror stillness. Purple-blue-black thunderheads roiling blue pond muddled with brown and yellow riffles on breezy autumn afternoon. Long navy blue shadows in rose-pink snow.

Sooty blue camp robber jay. Hot blue light in Indian child's hair or crow's feather.

Soft blue smudge of far mountains. Shocking blue sky juxtaposed with yellow cottonwood in October. Black-lashed blue Irish eyes smiling in wrinkled, suntanned face. Plum-fuzz blue of black Andrew's countenance. Milky blue layered on black in my old dog's patient eyes.

What's Up?

You ask. Well, I'm not sure I know or feel that I can answer with aplomb since the night a playful child coaxed me to a hillside in the dark (feeling like a fool) to view the star-strewn sky, hands and feet on the ground, head between my knees and looking up so that suddenly clutching at grass in panic desperately, with curled-down toes and tight-clenched hands, (lest I be dropped into icy darkness of interstellar space) I lost my sense of "what's up" and learned another meaning to "falling out!"

Photograph

What interpretation drain my soul to dryness and remain where I cannot, in some insane travesty of me; a shadow caught in light with permanency unsought? I pray in horror it will not. Let no shadow-light transpose to imagery that stays, bestows more immortality than creature knows. One instant held and magnified; by continuum verified? The quivering soul grows terrified: Hell could be this moment extracted; enacted, enacted, forever enacted, absolute truth of it exacted.

I forever I? In ultimate dread I shudder; with life uncoveted let live what does, and all that dies lie dead.

Cold War

Far in a mountain fastness, caved in ice and fury, Great Ursus shook himself and rumbled in his throat. Mountains trembled; crystals of symmetry, stained bloody red, spewed forth and petrified a world into a frozen sculpture of rigid attitude. Fragmented planet debris wove a net, encircled, captured this self-consciously pendant globe. (Once as a child I awoke to see sun-dogs ablaze in a misty sparkle of sky. Unhappy knowledge this: to see four minor suns escort the Unchanging across the winter morning. No less unnerving this: to feel the uncertainty of temporary moons.)

One knew, once, the sure solidity of earth; sun rising, setting, rising in endless unquestioned succession when up was up and down, down -- when heaven was one thing and hell another, and crucifixion was the only death to which God had been subjected.

Charlotte II

As spiders go, she was enormous. Her ambitious web from rosebush to rosebush spread its lovely concentric pattern, catching dewdrops and Japanese beetles, indiscriminately. And I liked her.

Now and again, for love, I gifted her with a fresh-caught beetle lunch. She darted out, wrapped it with silk most efficiently, hung it in her web for us both to admire. But not for long. Overcome by appetite, she sped along the shining thread to where it hung, her tight-wrapped prize, and quick and deft, she pierced it with a straw (that's how it looked to me!) and with gourmet delight, sipped the beetle dry. One night it rained and blew a fearsome gale, and then when morning came, I went to call, and found only a gaping hole in the air between the roses. My friend was gone. "Well, it was only a spider, for God's sake," they said. But I cried. They all think I'm crazy. But I wish I'd taken her picture while she lived between my roses.

Poppy In The Sun

Acquiescent poppy, passive receptacle open to quiet afternoon sun-strength emanations, sated, grows; and there is gratitude. O, Sun: Cease not to shine! Surround to fullest blossoming until poppy-crimson richness spills into muted shadows of evening.

Aspen

A slightest hint of breeze, a stir of air disturbs the slender aspen; agitates, sets leaves to shaking, trembling, a-quiver. Its slender trunk, suppliant, bends and turns. Not by coincidence the aspen grows sheltered by the tall, firm-rooted steadfastness of the hushing pine.

God, Make For Me A Buttercup

God, make for me a buttercup, color it bright and let me discover it at day's first light.

Make for me a daisy of lavender hue, yellow at the center, a posy true.

Make for me a poppy, a scarlet cup; with crystal dewdrops, fill it up.

Lily-of-the-valley make for me; carve its blossoms of ivory.

But first, buttercup and daisy so I can see if he likes butter, and if he likes me.

This land grieves. Do not suppose that trees along the Wind River are unaware of fires that consume forests of the Yellowstone.

Listen to the keening of the pines; and the grass is thirsty. Come, says God, let us reason together. Do you really believe you understand my creation better than I? Trees, too, are my creatures, and deer and elk and grass. Cry for them. Mourn their suffering and death. Sooner or later you will understand, with pain, what great, strong kinship I meant for you to have with them. The cowman knows.

Strange winds stir, stranger hues color the sunsets. Fires consume the forests; diesel exhaust and particulates ascend, descend -- portend something. Yet we believe we have in us the power to control. There is in us such unsound arrogance; "we create ourselves by choice from muck and mire, we have no need: none is higher than we in our intelligence."

Still, strange hues, strange stirrings of the air, consuming fires of forest and city; half-hidden apprehension, defiant uneasiness haunt the breeze. Mountains and prairies sigh, how long, O Lord. How long.

Reflection

Today I saw the death of a child; a boy. He was suddenly struck by a car on a gray-iced street. As in a fragment of a picture I saw with some strange, interrupted clarity, his hand, thin-wristed, curled, extending from the cuff of a green-plaid jacket: saw queer, congealing shapes of blood, live red, inexorably creeping across frozen slush: thought "But the street is too hard and cold." (surely a child seems entitled to warmer death. Skinned knees and hands seemed more indignity, when sidewalks were cold.)

I, a stranger, on that arrested moment gave birth to him, nurtured his growing, and was bereaved. At once I stand outside the event, considering. Often, I have thought about dying; today confronted, I think about death.

Certainty

A MAN IN SPACE!

The face of the world upturns to try to see an invisible mote afloat in the eye of the sky. A minute atom in the eternal object has momentarily escaped the motion of its predestined whirl (though still held within dimension.)

Grandfather patiently kneels; loosens the sweet-smelling ground round the reassuring roots of his unmoving roses.

Upper Country Panorama

Lushness of the valley floor, greens and greens of every shade and tone, excited now with yellows, calmed and soothed with gray, textured with sagebrush tufts or smooth and soft with cut-hay lands. Here and there stand cottonwoods, then pines and firs; summer-dark, deep-shadowed, follow the river-bank, cluster in groves. Blues and blues surround; green-blue, gray-blue, indigo cup this valley. Back drop of carven rock encloses valley floor; blue shadows dance with sunlight under passing cloud.

Sweetwater

A silent courage hovers over the boundless reaches of the great plateau, the Sweetwater.

It lingers in the infinite expanding sky. It moves in the restlessness of the eternal wind,

And we who love Wyoming receive it; a quiet benediction, bequeathed by those who found the waters sweet and blessed the good land wherein the waters flowed; bestowed upon all those who love the Sweetwater their inheritance of silent courage laid upon the great plateau.

One On The Right, One On The Left

Maria dolorosa, didst thou see? Were vision in the night surrounding thee? At the moment of conception, didst thou see?

Maria dolorosa, couldst thou hear? Did angel voices easy thy trembling fear? As thou acceptedst patient waiting, couldst thou hear?

Maria dolorosa, Didst thou know that to the cross thy son would surely go? In the hour of thy deliverance, didst thou know?

Maria dolorosa, At Simeon's word did thy heart rise up in pain and cry thy Lord that thy own side receive the piercing sword?

Maria dolorosa, thou couldst bear? As he grew to perfect manhood, didst prepare? Crucifixion find thee stronger than despair?

Maria dolorosa, in thy grief couldst thou give aught of thy faith and thy belief? Is there solace for the mother of the thief?

Let It Stand

Thoughts to record in ringing, resounding words
Before they disintegrate
Or float away, I write, erase, rewrite;
Scratch out, tear up,
Throw away.
Shades of Milton,
William Blake,
Lord Alfred, the
Brownings;
Rossetti, C. and D. G.,
And my jugged Persian friend,
stand at my shoulder.
"Do this. Do that."
Would a little of R _____ K _____ help?
Help! Help!
I once tried a bit of Dylan Thomas
But
I was confused, already.
Please, good critics (living yet
or long, long dead) bear with me.
What I write, I write, and I write what I think.
STET!

Printed in the United States
By Bookmasters